Product Overview

Fill 4 Will

An easy booklet for making your Will yourself

This booklet is an easy guide to make your will yourself. With the help of this booklet, you can easily understand 'How to make a will'. This booklet is divided into chapters, so that you can understand step by step process of making a will.

Disclaimer: But this booklet is not substituted of Advocates advice and it is highly recommended that after making a will with the help of this booklet, one should be reviewed by a practicing advocate once.

This booklet contains-

1. Booklet

2. Specimen Draft Will

3. Will Template

1 Booklet

Introduction to using this easy booklet

1.please read this booklet thoroughly.

2.Understand the specimen draft of will provided in the booklet to understand how your will is supposed to be written.

3.Fill in your details correctly and carefully in the draft will at all places which have been left blank for you to fill in your relevant information.

4. A Will can be made on the simple plain paper. No need of stamp paper.

5.Sign the filled draft will along with two witnesses and keep it at a safe place.

6.It is optional to register your will. You may choose to get your will registered at the sub-registrar office.

7. Please go through FAQs section before writing your will.

Frequently asked questions

Making of will

1. What is a will?

A will is a legal declaration on a plain paper by a person of his or her intention and desire of how his or her asset is to be dealt with or disposed of after the person's death. Will can be changed at anytime or withdrawn during the lifetime of the person making the will even if it is registered.

2. Who can make a will?

Any person- man or woman -having age of 18 or above with sound mind can make a will.

3. When should I make a will?

No age limit or perfect age of making a will. After 18 year, you can make a will. It is advisable that when you start earning and acquiring some assets you must start making a will.

4. Do I need lawyer to make my will?

No, it is up to you. you can make your will yourself.

5. Does will have to be on stamp paper?

No, will on plain paper be valid.

6. Is it compulsory to register the will?

No, it is desirable.

7. Why should I make a will?

In the absence of a Will, your asset may go to someone who you don't expect or want it to go to. if you have minor children, then under a will you can **appoint a guardian** who will take care of your children in case of your unfortunate death. if you die without a will, the court appoints a guardian, who you may not have Wanted.

under a will you can decide who will be the **executor** or the person who will oversee the disposal of your assets after your death .in the absence of will, the court appoints an administrator, who you may not have wanted. you can name **alternate beneficiaries** in your will in the event the main beneficiary also dies with or before you. Having a proper will may avoid disputes between persons who claim a right to your asset. It is possible to give your share of the coparcenary asset through a will, which would otherwise go to the other member of the coparcenary, including your children.

8. How can I revoke or amend my will?

It is up to you(testator). You can change, amend, revoke your will at any time.

9. Where should I keep my will?

You can keep your will anywhere as your wish. But it is advisable that you store it in a secure and a safe place where it cannot tamper or lost. you can keep it in a bank locker or in registrar office. some financial institution and the bank also provide custodian services for safekeeping of wills.

Appointment of the Executor

10. Who is an executor?

One who execute your will. The executor is the legal representative for all purposes of a deceased person (testator) and all the property of the testator vests in him.

11. Is it mandatory to appoint an Executor?

No, but it is advisable to appoint an executor.

12. Can I appoint my relative or friend as an Executor?

Yes

13. Can I appoint any beneficiary as an Executor?

Yes

14. Who is Residuary legatee?

After distribution of property in Will, one who gets balance property.

Beneficiary

15. Can I exclude my immediate family members as beneficiaries?

Yes

16. Is beneficiary and nominee same?

No, nominee is only a trustee of the property whereas beneficiary is entitled to get the property under the will.

Witnesses

17. Why witnesses needed?

A witness attests the will and assures that the testator was mentally fit and has freely (without any coercion, undue influence) written the Will.

18. Who can be a witness?

Any adult person -man or women- of 18 year can be a witness. It is inevitable that they must not be a beneficiary in written Will.

Registration of will

19. Is it compulsory to register Will?
No, optional

Asset and property

20. Which kind of property can be mentioned in the will?
Self -earned and self- acquired property, ancestral properties in which title or ownership are legally transferred, your share in a business, property situated in abroad can be bequeathed.

21. Can a share in HUF be bequeathed?

No

22. Can rented property be bequeathed?

No

Probate

23. What is probate?

Probate means a copy of the will, certified under the seal of competent court with a grant of administration of the estate to the executor of the testator. It is the official evidence of an executor's authority.

2 Sketch of will

A will can be divided into the following parts

Introduction

In this part, your name, father's name, place of residence, is to be written

Declaration

in this part you declare about status of your health and your consent, and if you have made a will or codicil before it, then it is mentioned that it is cancelled and withdrawn.

Family details

In this part, the name of your family members, your relationship with them, your marriage status etc. are mentioned.

Main part
(Distribution of Property)

In this section you are mentioned how are you sharing your property

The recipients of the **residuary legatee**

Who will get the remaining portion of your property, it is mentioned?

Executor

In this section you name the execution and alternative performance of your choice

Witness 1

The name and address of the witness who verifies the signatory's signature

Witness 2

The name and address of the witness who verifies the signature of the will.

(*For this there is no canonical format by law, this is a model and it can be adjusted accordingly*)

How to make a Will?

Example- Ramesh Mishra is working in a bank. His wife Jaya Mishra is a housewife. He has two children, Raju Mishra and Priya Mishra. Ramesh is of 46 year of age and he wants to make his will. How Ramesh makes his will, let's see-

Rough work- First of all Ramesh fill up the blanks given and make a list of his personal statements, all the assets and the ones he wants to give.

1. Full legal name ...*Ramesh Mishra*......

2. Father's name ..*Jairam Mishra*.....

3. Gender ...*male*.......

4. Religions...*Hindu*.....

    Note: - Because the personal law is different, rules of will are changed.

5. Business/occupation ..*Bank manager*. ...

6. Date of birth/age..*27-6-1972*.........

7. Address of residence .... *House no.123, star city Lucknow, Uttar Pradesh* ....

8   Marital status .... *married*......

9   Married then the full name of ~~husband~~/wife.......... *Jaya Mishra age 44 years*....

10 Your children or family members details, their name/age....... *Raju Mishra, 25 years, Priya Mishra 23 years*............

11 Whom want to appoint an Executor: - Name / Address / Relationship / Age .. *Jaya Mishra (wife)*.....

12 Whom Want to appoint an Alternate Executor: - Name / Address / Relationship / Age .... *Amit Mehta s/o Krishna Mehta, star city Lucknow Uttar Pradesh.*

13. Who will be the Residuary legatee: - Name / address / relationship .. *Jaya Mishra (wife)*....

Property distribution

Particulars of property		Beneficiary details		
Type of property	property details	Name	Relation	Address
Self-made property	House no.123, star city, Lucknow, UP	Jaya Mishra	Wife	House no.123, star city, Lucknow, Uttar Pradesh.
Share in inheritance property	300 sq. feet share in 1200 sq. feet of land at Kajubagan, Lucknow	Jaya Mishra	Wife	House no.123, star city, Lucknow, Uttar Pradesh.
Gold/jewelry	100g gold, which is in a locker at SBI kachahri branch Lucknow	Priya Mishra	Daughter	House no.123, star city, Lucknow, Uttar Pradesh.
Motor vehicle	Maruti car, model Alto, Vehicle no. UP2B-1001	Raju Mishra	Son	House no.123, star city, Lucknow, Uttar Pradesh.

Bank account locker etc.	5 lakh rupees deposited in A/C no 1234567890 at SBI, kachahri branch, Lucknow, UP	Jaya Mishra	Wife	House no.123, star city, Lucknow, Uttar Pradesh.
cash	5 lakhs in bedroom's Almirah	Jaya Mishra	Wife	House no.123, star city, Lucknow, Uttar Pradesh.
PPF/Gratuity	the sum of amount in PPF account	Jaya Mishra	Wife	House no.123, star city, Lucknow, Uttar Pradesh.
Insurance policy	LIC policy No.123456789	Raju Mishra	Son	House no.123, star city, Lucknow, Uttar Pradesh.
Share/ mutual fund	HDFC mid-cap fund, folio no.1232323456	Raju Mishra	Son	House no.123, star city, Lucknow, Uttar Pradesh.
Share in business	******	******	******	*****
others	******	Jaya Mishra	Wife	House no.123, star city, Lucknow, Uttar Pradesh.

(Fill in the blanks and your Will be ready)

Specimen

Date...9 February 2019.....

Last will and Testament of Mr. / ~~Mrs.~~ Ramesh Mishra

I....... *Ramesh Mishra*...., son / daughter /wife...*Jairam Mishra*.... Aged .*46*......., years, By religion...··*Hindu* ....Business/ occupation ....*Bank manager.*... , presently residing at.........*House no.123, star city, Lucknow, Uttar Pradesh.*........

Hereby declare that I am executing this will in complete possession of my physical and mental health and in a composed state of mind, without any coercion, compulsion or misrepresentation. I am making this will so that after my death no dispute remain amongst my family members, and it is my wish that after my death my will is acted upon by my family members in its true spirit. I declare to have fully understood its content and implications.

I also declare that this is to be my last will and testament and I revoke all my former wills, codicils made by me.

Family details

I am married / ~~unmarried~~ when making this will…………………I have two children Raju Mishra son age 25 residing at, star city Lucknow, Uttar Pradesh, and Priya Mishra, age 23, residing at, star city Lucknow Uttar Pradesh…………

Distribution of property

I wish that all my movable and immovable properties should be distributed in the following manner: -

S.N	Property/ Assets Description		Beneficiary Details			Remarks
	Assets Type	Details	Name	Relationship	Address	
1.	Self-made property	House no.123, Star city, Lucknow up	Jaya Mishra	wife	House no.123, star city, Lucknow, UP	

2	Share in inheritance property	300 sq. feet share in 1200 sq. feet of land at Kaju bagan, Lucknow	Jaya Mishra	wife	House no.123, star city, Lucknow, Uttar Pradesh	
3	Gold / Jewelry	100g of gold, which is in a locker at SBI, kachahri branch, Lucknow	Priya Mishra	Daughter	House no.123, star city, Lucknow, Uttar Pradesh	
4	Motor vehicle	Maruti car model-Alto, vehicle no-UP2B-1001	Raju Mishra	son	House no.123, star city, Lucknow, Uttar Pradesh	
5	Bank account, locker etc.	5 lakh rupees deposited at A/Cno.1234567890 at SBI, kachahri branch, Lucknow, UP	Jaya Mishra	wife	House no.123, star city, Lucknow, Uttar Pradesh	

6	cash	5 lakhs in Godrej's almirah (locker) in bedroom	Jaya Mishra	wife	House no-123, star city, Lucknow, Uttar Pradesh	
7	PPF/Gratuity	Sum of amount in PPF account	Jaya Mishra	wife	House no-123, star city, Lucknow, Uttar Pradesh	
8	Insurance policy	LIC policy No- 123456789	Raju Mishra	son	House no-123, star city, Lucknow, Uttar Pradesh	
9	Share in business	*********	******	*********	********	*******
10	Share/mutual fund	HDFC mid cap fund, folio no 1232323456	Raju Mishra	son	House no-123, star city, Lucknow, Uttar Pradesh	

| 11 | others | ***** | Jaya Mishra | wife | House no.123, star city, Lucknow, Uttar Pradesh | |
| 12 | ************ | ********* | ******* | ******** | ******* | ********* |

Executor Nomination

I appoint …Jaya Mishra… (my wife) ……. ………. son/daughter of ………. aged…44……….years, presently residing at……House no, 123, star city Lucknow, Uttar Pradesh………. as the executor of my will.

If for any reason the above executor is disabled or not interested or if he dies before me, **I** appoint …Amit Mehta……. son/daughter of…Krishna Mehta…….. aged…50……….years, presently residing at…star city Lucknow, Uttar Pradesh…… as the **alternative executor** of my will.

The executor will divide the property according to the instructions given in my will and pay the dues, fees, taxes etc. advanced on me. At the same time, the executor can take all the measures in relation to the arrears (including the interest which was decided between me and the debtors) which I have to take.

If there is some legal expenditure incurred by the execution of the above action, it can be reimbursed from my property.

Declaration

I, hereby declare that I am execution this will in complete possession of my physical and mental health and in a composed state of mind, without any coercion, compulsion undue influence or misrepresentation. I am making this will so that after my death no dispute will remain amongst my family members, and it is my wish that after my death my will is acted upon by my family members in its true spirit. I declare to have fully understood its content and implications.

Ramesh mishra

Date: *09/02/2019*……

Place: *Star city Lucknow Uttar Pradesh*………

Verification by witnesses

Witness 1

I, …*Ramakant Sharma s/o Prakash Sharma* resident of *star city Lucknow* by profession ……. *Doctor*……. have witnessed the signature of this will and affirm that the Testator appeared to me to be of sound mind, was not under duress, and the Testator affirmed to me that he/~~she~~ was aware of the nature of this will and signed it freely and voluntarily.

Ramakant Sharma

Date: *9/2/2019*

place: *star city Lucknow*

Witness 2

I, …*Srimati puja Mahajan*… w/o *Nitesh Mahajan* resident of *shivnagar*, *Lucknow*………by profession …*Banker*……. have witnessed the signature of this will and affirm that the Testator appeared to me to be of sound mind, was not under duress, and the Testator affirmed to me that he/~~she~~ was aware of the nature of this will and signed it freely and voluntarily.

Puja mahajan

Date: *9/2/2019*

Place ; *shivnagar, lucknow*

3 Will Template

For rough work

1. Full legal name ....

2. Father's names ....…

3. Gender ……………………….

4. Religions…....................
   Note: - Because the personal law is different, rules of will are changed.

5. Business/occupation…... ...

6. Date of birth/age………………………………….. ..

7. Address of residence ……………………....…….. ..

8. Marital status ………………………………….. ...

9. Married than full legal name of husband/wife
....

10. your children or family details Name/age ....
....
....

....
....

11 Whom want to appoint an executor: Name/Relationship/age..
....
....

12 Whom Want to appoint an Alternate Executor: - Name / Address / Relationship / Age
....
....
....

13 Who will be the Residuary legatee: - Name / address / relationship
....
....
....
....

Distribution of property

Type of property		Beneficiary details		
Type of property	Property details	Name	Relation	Address
self- made property				
share in inheritance property				
Gold/jewelry				
motor vehicle				

Bank account/locker etc.				
cash				
PPF/Gratuity				
insurance policy				
Share/mutual fund				

Share in business				
furniture				
others				

Now Fill in the blanks and your legal binding your WILL be ready

Date ………

Last will and Testament of MR. / MRs…….

I,…………………………….son/daughter/wife…..………………………………… ………………………………………………Aged…………………………..………… years…………………………………….. by religion……………………... Business/occupation……...…………………………….presently residing at…….………………………………………………………………………… ………………………………………………………………………………

Hereby declare that I am executing this will in complete possession of my physical and mental health and in a composed state of mind, without any coercion, compulsion or misrepresentation. I am making this will so that after my death no dispute remain amongst my family members, and it is my wish that after my death my will is acted upon by my family members in its true spirit. I declare to have fully understood its content and implications.

I also declare that this is to be my last will and testament and I revoke all my former wills, codicils made by me.

Family details

I am married / unmarried when making this will. I have Children/Family members ....

....

....

....

....

....

....

....

....

I wish that all my movable and immovable properties should be distributed in the following manner: -

Distribution of property

Property /Assets Description		Beneficiary Details			Remarks
Assets Type	Details	Name	Relationship	Address	

Distribution of property

Property/ Assets Description			Beneficiary Details			Remarks
	Assets Type	Details	Name	Relationship	Address	

Distribution of property

Property/Assets Description		Beneficiary Details			Remarks
Assets Type	Details	Name	Relationship	Address	

Distribution of property

Property/Assets Description		Beneficiary Details			Remarks
Assets Type	Details	Name	Relationship	Address	

Executor Nomination

I appoint ………………………………………………………………………… son/daughter of………………………………………….aged…………………..years presently residing at………………………………………………………………………………………………

………………………………………………………………………………………………………

………………………………………………………………………………………………………

………………… as the Executor of my will.

If for any reason the above Executor is disabled or not interested or if he dies before me, **I** appoint …………………………………………….son/daughter of………………………………………………………………………………………………… aged………………..years, presently residing at … …………………………………….

………………………………………………………………………………………………………

………………………………………………………………………………………………………

………………… as the Alternative Executor of my will.

The executor will divide the property according to the instructions given in my will and pay the dues, fees, taxes etc. advanced on me. At the same time, the executor can take all the measures in relation to the arrears (including the interest which was decided between me and the debtors) which I have to take. If there is some legal expenditure incurred by the execution of the above action, it can be reimbursed from my property.

Declaration

I, hereby declare that I am execution this will in complete possession of my physical and mental health and in a composed state of mind, without any coercion, compulsion undue influence or misrepresentation. I am making this will so that after my death no dispute will remain amongst my family members, and it is my wish that after my death my will is acted upon by my family members in its true spirit. I declare to have fully understood its content and implications.

Signature

Name ....
Date ....
Place ....

Verification by witnesses

Witness 1

I,..S/o,D/o,W/o........................
....resident of..
....
by profession.................................have witnessed the signature of this will and affirm that the Testator appeared to me to be of sound mind,

was not under duress, and the Testator affirmed to me that he/she was aware of the nature of this will and signed it freely and voluntarily.

Signature -

Date:

place:

Witness 2

I,……………………………………………………………S/o,D/o,W/o………………….………………………………………………………………………………………..resident of…… by profession………………………......………..have witnessed the signature of this will and affirm that the Testator appeared to me to be of sound mind, was not under duress, and the Testator affirmed to me that he/she was aware of the nature of this will and signed it freely and voluntarily.

Signature -

Date:

place:

Finally, sign each and every page with two witnesses. Put your will in an envelope and seal, that's it.

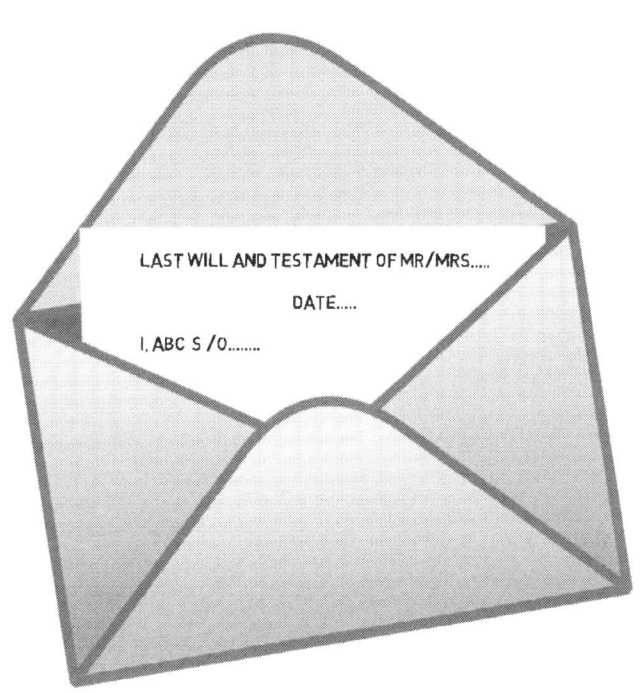

Wish you all the best

Made in the USA
Columbia, SC
29 April 2025

57307884R00024